Red and Yellow Leaves

Artem Vaskanyan

Cadmus Publishing
www.cadmuspublishing.com

Copyright © 2023 Artem Vaskanyan

Cover art by Edgar Vaskanyan

Published by Cadmus Publishing
www.cadmuspublishing.com
Port Angeles, WA

ISBN: 978-1-63751-349-1

All rights reserved. Copyright under Berne Copyright Convention, Universal Copyright Convention, and Pan-American Copyright Convention. No part of this book may be reproduced, stored in a retrieval system, or transmitted in any form, or by any means, electronic, mechanical, photocopying, recording or otherwise, without prior permission of the author.

Acknowledgments

I would first like to thank my brother for his support and his beautiful artwork. More of my brother's artwork can be viewed on his Instagram: Edgar Vaskanyan Art Studio. Next, I would like to thank my yoga instructor, Angela Cote for the teachings and support. Thank you to my close friend Amos Don, who is the author of a beautiful poetry book, "My Blue Days Sound Like Blue Jays," and his lady, Joanna for her help.

Thank you also to Nahomie Vilnaigre who is an author of a Haitian Bilingual Book for children, "Lili, Grandma, and Legume." A special thank you to Boston University for providing education at Norfolk Prison and to all of my professors who contributed to bringing education; Thank you Professor Anne Blackwill, Patrick Conway, Scott Reuscher, Jake Bower-Bir, Karen Lachinsky, Dev Luthra, Lee Pearlman, Andre DeQuadros, Jamie Hillman, Shelly Tenebaum, Abraham Waya, Gary Donato, Jenifer Drew, Mary Allen Mastrorilli, and to Junot Diaz for his inspiration.

I would also like to thank James Martin, Ronald Leftwich, Wayne Grant, Nathan Rivera, and Timothy Miller for their constructive criticism; and to all real Convicts in Norfolk prison who supported and were happy for me. Thank you all so much!

To the Readers

"Red and Yellow Leaves," has taken an entire four seasons to complete, during which time I reflected on my life through the Yoga Sutra and Buddhist "Zen" meditation practices. My self-reflection increased my self-awareness and has forced me to express my ruminating thoughts through poetry, even if I, in the process, had to insult amongst others myself to get my message across; since my dislike for the hypocrites is just as strong as it is for the wicked.

Please keep in mind that some of my poetry can be offensive. If I managed to create with some of my poems, an empowering, or a pleasant feeling, or stir emotions of disgust and anger, then I have fulfilled my purpose as a poet.

In order to create empowering poetry that could move my readers, I had to put aside my personal opinions of what other people might think of me. I needed to make a self-sacrifice to get my point across. If I was to care about other's feelings while creating poetry, then all of my work would have been subjective, and I would be a fraud and a fool to try to please everyone.

Poetry is an art,
And an art has no place
For cowards, frauds, and fools.

ALSO BY ARTEM VASKANYAN:

RUMINATING YEARS

ZEK (THE CONVICT)

Red and Yellow Leaves

-are the reminders that all is temporal

For Family

Since what are we without it?

Nothing more than a single red-yellow leaflet

Holding on to its dear life

To a stem of a tree,

-Artem Vaskanyan

TABLE OF CONTENTS

Book I: First Days of Autumn 1
Book II: Last Days of Winter. 79
Book III: When Lilacs Blossom 153
Book IV: Dark Cave. 197

Book I

First Days of Autumn

ARTEM VASKANYAN

Book I Contents

First Days of Autumn. 4
Only a Beginning! 5
No Love 6
A Thought of Loneliness 7
We Are Like Fish 8
An Empty Void 9
A Dream. 10
Freedom 11
My Selfish Nature 12
One Look 13
A Cockroach 14
Until 15
My Cell 16
What keeps me.... 17
Two Spirits 18
Brother 19
An Evil Spirit 20
I thought to Myself.... .21
Two Men 23
In My Dreams... 24
The Meeting. 25
I am a Mountain! 26
Regular Folks 27
Hot as Hell 28
A Hell of a Reason 30
A Bad Day. 31
Equally Balanced 32
Our Senses 33
It was Not... 34
Politicians 35
Disgusting Feeling. 36
You are your Spirit 37
The Words. 38
Not in Vain 39

RED AND YELLOW LEAVES

Avaricious Men	40
Never Forget	41
Know how it Feels	42
Death	43
Despair	44
In Debt with the Devil	45
An Open Manhole	46
Set in Motion	47
As of Yet	49
The Chickens	50
Freethinker	51
My Animal Instinct	53
Folks Like Me	55
RED	56
The Only Question	58
Fifty-Three!	59
When they Came…	60
Refined	62
A Melancholic Heart	63
You can have it All!	64
Out of my Control	65
Drop Your Act	66
Alone	67
A Blessing	68
How can you say	69
The Best Years	70
Ground of Belief	71
The Trash	72
Ignorance	73
The Vagabond	74
My heart lied	75
Fate	76
Outside These Walls	77

ARTEM VASKANYAN

First Days of Autumn

First days of Autumn
Are the best days out of the whole year
for me,
because that is when I get to see,
the leaves of the trees
turn red-yellow color,
the color of my favored precious metal
That is!
For when I look at trees
with red-yellow leaves,
 As if they are made out of gold,
It all of the sudden starts to dwell on me
of how similar it is
to all life in the temporal world.
The beauty of life is like real gold,
that all life finds itself indulging in
when it is at its fullest.
But as life gradually comes to an end
just like every season,
it tries to avoid at any cost,
to deal with,
when it starts to change for the worst.
First days of Autumn
are a wake-up call for me,
for it makes me become aware even more
that life as I know is getting shorter
by each passing Autumn season.
And soon, I will be hanging on
to my last breath,
just like a last red-yellow leaflet,
hanging desperately on to a naked stem of a tree,
for its dear life,
At the end of each Autumn season.

2021

ONLY A BEGINNING!

It is all only a beginning!
Not sure exactly why I said
these words to my old friend.
Perhaps I wanted to sound poetic
when everyone around us
were drained out of life,
and that there must be a deeper meaning
to this wretched life
that now is installed for me.
Or perhaps, it was not even I who said these words,
but my disappointed spirit with me
who wanted much more for me out of life,
then this soul-ravaged future life
that I have created,
and who simply could not accept the fact
that there will not be a happy ending
after all for me.

No Love

The way you love your young,
is the way they will love you
when you are old.
I wish you would have known that
when I was young,
for now that you are old,
I barely feel any love for you.

A Thought of Loneliness

I feel my bones shiver,
from a thought of loneliness.
I look around and to my left,
I see a sunset starts to emerge,
behind the trees.
To my right, I see the Watch Tower,
and the guard inside polishing his rifle.
I look up, and see the cloudless blue sky,
and a pair of hawks fly over me.
(Damn! How I wish to be one of them).
I look down to my feet
and see that I am standing on a dried-up grass.
I do not even bother to look straight ahead
to see that soul-crushing wall
that is keeping me inside.
Nor do I bother looking over my shoulder
to see the prison block
where I ruminate at night on a thought of loneliness.
I close my eyes,
slowly exhale to my last sigh.
I raise my head and look up
into a cloudless blue sky,
and pray to be set free one day.

ARTEM VASKANYAN

WE ARE LIKE FISH

We are like fish
who do not know that they are
in the water,
until they are pulled out of it.
We think that our fishpond
is all there is to this world,
until we see the other ponds,
and only then we start to realize
how close minded we all have been.

An Empty Void

Is this all there is to your life?
Eat, defecate, sleep, and fornicate.
Then your so-called life I must say,
is empty!
And living an empty life
is like standing on the edge of the precipice,
waiting to fall into oblivion.
You must be at least feeling it in your heart
as night after night is passing,
that life without a purpose
is truly meaningless,
unless you start to ruminate on the Self
by digging deep into the heart of your soul,
to overcome fear from uncovering
the hidden dark memories.
Face your fears do not be afraid,
or ashamed to embrace your new Self
who desperately is striving to begin
by filling in with purpose an empty void.

A Dream

There is a dream that feels like a nightmare
that keeps re-visiting me every night,
where I walk alone in the dark forest,
lost, confused, hungry, and cold.
Only the full moon above the top of the trees
illuminating me and giving me hope
to find my path.
I walk in circles as it appears
without finding my way out of the dark forest,
and every time it starts to feel
that I come closer to discovering my path,
there is some kind of mischievous spirit
that wakes me up,
and I return bewildered to the world that I came from.
I desperately await the night to approach
so, I could fall asleep and search for my dream
in hopes to find my way
out of the dark forest.
For I feel as if my spirit
is trapped in my dream,
in the dark forest,
and I must search until I will find my way
to reconnect with my lost spirit.

Freedom

To all who are oppressed, I say
get mad more often at the way
you are being treated by your oppressors!
Once freedom starts to fade away
and you do not put up a fight to stop it,
then your life will never be the same
for you will start to wither away
without it.
When you hear people say,
"Hide your anger, your frustration,
do not let others see your emotions arise,"
Then that is how you know
who your oppressors are.
I say, express your anger,
your frustrations and emotions
without fear and shame,
because that is how a free man
should feel and act.
For a man was a created free
and only the Creator can take
the freedom away from thee.
I say, no man can ever take
the freedom from another,
he can only make him surrender it.

2021

My Selfish Nature

It was never about helping others
even though many times I said
that it was.
Everything that I ever did was
for myself and myself only.
My altruistic behavior was
nothing more than a farce
in disguise.
In truth, it was never about us,
it was only about me,
And that is just how my nature,
your nature, all of our nature, is.
Anyone who portrays to be other than that
is one big fat hypocrite.
For he or she knows better than I do
that the sole difference between us
is that I am not ashamed to admit
the selfish nature that lives in all of us.
Even admitting this truth,
is really not about the truth
but to make me face myself
so "I" could internally grow.

ONE LOOK

One look is all it took
for me to see the person
that she is.
Nothing more than a rot,
a poisonous snake that swims in the swamp,
and if I would have ignored
what my heart had whispered
to my soul,
then I too would have suffered
just like many others do
when they fall victim
to her poisonous charms.

A Cockroach

At times I feel like a cockroach
who never gives up.
No matter how many times
I have been stepped on, beat down,
dehumanized, oppressed, depressed,
and forced myself to forget the rest…
I just will not go away and die!
I get back on my feet
and start moving forward again.
I live my life like a cockroach,
because in the end a cockroach
always survives.

UNTIL

Fight is not considered to be a fight,
until you fight to your last breath.
Loneliness is not considered to be loneliness,
until the only person that you know
is yourself.
Mistake is not considered to be a mistake,
until you are paying for it
with your life.
Hunger is not considered to be hunger,
until you start to think about
the last meal you had.
Starvation is not considered to be starvation,
until the only food that is left
is you.
Hate is not considered to be hate
until you start to seek revenge.
Revenge is not considered to be revenge,
until you and your enemy are both
in the grave.
Love is not considered to be love,
until your life feels meaningless
without your loved one.

My Cell

My cell is my temple!
It is sacred!
And it is not just four brick walls
that keep me confined.
My cell is a place
where I nurture my body,
cultivate my mind and soul,
and test the strength of my spirit,
and where I find peace and quiet
in times of turmoil and upheaval.
My cell is sacred!
It is my sanctuary!
Where, during despair and loss,
I find a way to blossom
even without a drop of rain.

WHAT KEEPS ME...

What keeps me ticking forward
like a grandfather clock,
is to make my dreams a reality,
and in the process,
turn all of those with whom I shared
my fruitful visions,
into believers,
and that it is only men
who hold on to their dreams,
can make them a reality.

2021

Two Spirits

When a good spirit fails at its task
and the wicked man sees it,
then his spirit will suddenly arise
to indulge with pleasure of his failures.
The self-gratification
that the wicked spirit receives
when it sees a good man fail,
is exactly alike, but only in a good way
when a good man sees
a wicked spirit fails.

BROTHER

Brother!
We were created out of the same ingredients
and yet we are nothing alike.
We both desire and dream of life
different from each other.
Our spirits have nothing in common
and we could not understand each other.
Until both of our souls have been fractured
by the obstacles of life.

An Evil Spirit

There is an evil spirit
that lives in all of us,
that comes to life
when we ignore our virtue,
and after the evil spirit
is done with us
and we come back to our senses,
we start to realize
that living life under a rock
like some kind of insect
was not all that bad.
For when we let an evil spirit arise
and dominate our mind,
it violated our entire body
and left our soul fractured and abandoned
without a roof over our head
to sleep peacefully at night.

2021

I Thought to Myself...

I wish you would've kept your mouth shut
and never revealed what lurks
deep down in your heart.
For when you opened your mouth
and words began to flow,
right there and then I thought to myself...
"Why are you revealing your wicked deeds to me?
I do not want to know
about them nor your pain and suffering
that you endure because of your bad karma.
I can barely deal with my own cause and effect.
I have no place in me to take yours in
and ruminate on them
when I have not even grasped my own.
You are just like a caught fish in the net,
grasping for a drink of water
when you are pulled out of the lake.
But I have no water to share with you,
I barely have enough to drink myself.
Do not think for a second
that by sharing your wicked deeds with me,
you would set yourself free
by making peace with yourself.
For it is not what you say that matters
but what you do in the present
that will bring change
to your future affects by your karma.
I do not have a single thought of sympathy
for someone like you
who knew that he was living a rotten life
since he could remember,
and yet persisted to continue to cultivate the wickedness in his heart.
How can you look directly in my eyes
and say,
'I deserve your sympathy!'

When you have never done a single act
to change your karma
by abolishing your wickedness?"

2021

Two Men

There is a difference between two men,
the difference between a sane and an insane man.
The so called sane, a "normal man,"
appears to hold himself better in control
when shit hits the fan.
While the so called insane, a "mad man,"
lets all of his emotions flow
without considering what others may think
of his words and actions.
Even though a "mad man"
will never admit his lunacy amongst the normal men,
since, in his self-obsessed mind's eye,
he is not doing anything wrong
besides being true to himself.
But that does not mean
that a "normal man,"
does not have what it takes
to act like a "mad man,"
For when there are no eyes on him,
he reveals, and only to himself,
the crazy nature that he conceals
behind closed doors from other men.
Thus, the difference between two men,
is that one thinks and acts aloud
while the other keeps it all in
when these two men have eyes on them.

2021

In My Dreams…

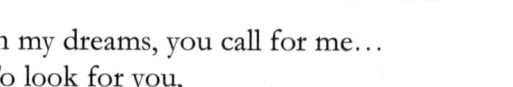

In my dreams, you call for me…
To look for you,
So, you could look into my eyes,
when I find you,
and reveal your soul to me
so, I would give my heart to you.

The Meeting

I run as fast as I can
to the East.
To meet my Creator
with a loud yell…
For my Father Sky!
For my Mother Earth!
To hear that I am coming
over the mountains,
and greet my Creator
before the first light emerges
over the vast forests of mountains.

I am a Mountain!

I am a mountain!
I cannot be moved.
I will not be moved.
My mind is still.
My breath is steady.
My heart beats with the rhythm.
My eyes are slightly open and locked in
on a spot three feet in front of me.
My mouth is slightly open
with a steady breath.
My back is straight.
My shoulders slightly tilted back.
My legs are in a full lotus
and my hands are placed on top of my knees.
I take a deep breath in
and slowly exhale
and then I do that three more times,
and on my last
I send the breath down below my naval,
where I hold it in for an entire minute.
I then slowly exhale
to my last drop of air in me
and in the process, I let go
of everything that tormented me.
I am a mountain!
I cannot be moved.
I will not be moved.
My mind is still.
My breath is steady.
My heart beats with the rhythm.
And my Spirit
is stagnant like a lake
by the mountain.

2021

Regular Folks

The more I encounter deeply religious folks,
particularly here with me in prison,
the more I become certain
that it is not for me.
For these folks
I consider to be extremely dangerous.
For as they search for the One,
and when they supposedly do find Him,
they put all of their eggs
into one special basket,
and when this basket one day is dropped,
then their entire life savings is shattered.
On Saturdays and particularly on Sundays,
I find them to be at their best
with the big smile on their faces
and with the Big Book in their hands,
but on any other day of the week
they are just like regular folks,
Full of bullshit.

2021

ARTEM VASKANYAN

Hot as Hell

That day it was hot as Hell!
The air was muggy,
it was difficult to breath,
the windows were…
Well!
There were no windows in no ones' cell,
only a trap window
in the solid metal closed cell door.
(A sudden utter!)
A pinching sound echoed across
the silent tear on the second floor.
The pain felt real
like it was mine,
exuded from the core of another
prisoner's soul.
No one could see his eyes
to tell the pain that he was in
behind the closed metal cell doors,
and no one needed to
To know what truly lied
deep down in his core.
For it was obvious to everyone.
For we all felt what he felt
deep down in our souls.
The loathe for the men who kept us
trapped worse than animals,
was consuming each and every one of us
in the same way.
And I, fought many internal battles
with all my soul
to resist this loathing temptation.
Some I won and some I lost.
Nevertheless, I kept feeding my mind
with positive thoughts.
"Nothing is permanent.

RED AND YELLOW LEAVES

Not even this living Hell!"
I know from my personal experience,
how easy it was to feed the hatred
that lives inside us all,
For I saw and encountered many men
who spent many months in the living Hell
with the eyes beyond healing.
And, if there ever once lived
a kind spirit in them,
it had left them a long time ago,
from living in a place
that was as hot as Hell.

2021

A Hell of a Reason

There must be a hell of a reason,
why life on earth was created for men
to be full of pain and suffering.
I cannot help but to ask myself,
"Can you imagine living an easy life?
So easy that no man
will ever have to endure
any pain or suffering?
Then this kind of life
would be meaningless.
For an easy life
does not evolve a man,
it does not make him grow
spiritually and intellectually.
Those who have managed to alleviate their lives with wealth
from the sufferings of life,
no matter how spiritual and intellectual
they claim to be,
will never pray to The Creator
with all their soul,
not like a man who knows
the true meaning of pain and suffering.
For a man who endured
the perpetual sufferings of life on his own mind and flesh,
is unequivocally more profound with life experience
in every way.
For when he prays,
he prays with every living atom in his soul.
And when he speaks of life,
he speaks from the heart.
And those whose pain and suffering do not come close to his
cannot resist but to indulge in his words."

2021

A Bad Day

The only thing that I'm sure about
in life,
One hundred and ten percent,
is that early tomorrow morning,
the sun will rise,
And at night,
the Moon and then the Stars,
will mysteriously appear,
and I will briefly pray.
Everything else besides that
on a bad day,
is cloudy,
like a glass of milk.

2021

Equally Balanced

The suffering that is endured
by a man in life
has to be sufficient.
It has to be equally balanced,
just like justice,
or it will butcher a man's mind
to the point of beyond repair.

2021

Our Senses

When it is murky outside
and we fail to see clearly
what transpires on our path,
then it is in our innate human nature
to use the rest of our senses,
Smell, hear, taste, touch
to explain to ourselves
what we cannot comprehend,
and if they fairly fail as well,
then the sixth sense
suddenly will come to light,
to guide us through our dark path.

It was Not...

It was not your family who mistreated you.
It was not you who committed the crime.
It was not the cops who illegally arrested you.
It was not the prosecutor who sought the harshest
prison sentence again you.
It was not the informant who falsely testified against you.
It was not the victims who desperately wanted
revenge against you.
It was not the biased jury who found you guilty.
It was not the judge's arrogance who cruelly sentenced you.
It was not the Correctional Officers who insulted
and sadistically tormented you.
It was not society who rejected you.
It was not the court or the parole board
who refused to give you a second chance.
It was, however, the ideology,
and it was the only culprit here.

Politicians

You say you care!
You say you want to help!
You say you give a damn!
Well, here I am!
I am begging on my knees for your help!
What else do you need to hear?
What else do you need to see
for you to realize that your words
are meaningless to me?
Without actions, there is no help!
You say you care!
You say you want to help!
You say you give a damn!
Well, look at me!
I am trapped!
I cannot breathe without the help!
And all I hear from you
are more false promises that you will come and help!
I do not know what else to do!
How else do I say this to you
for you to turn your words
into some actions?
Unless you are waiting for me to die,
and then come out and say,
"How come you did not ask for my help
when you needed help?"

Disgusting Feeling

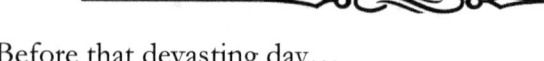

Before that devasting day…
I woke up with a disgusting feeling in my gut
in the middle of the night,
like my happy and ignorant life
was about to come to an end.
Every atom in my body told me
to get up! Pack my stuff!
and get on the road
as quickly as I could
without ever looking back.
I chose not to listen to my gut
that eerie day,
and because of that,
I pay dearly with my life
till this very day.
Where since that day…
instead of getting tipsy off Armenian red wine,
I now get the buzz from drinking cheap black tea,
write poetry all night under the moonlight,
ruminate relentlessly on life,
and pay attention
to the disgusting feelings in my gut
that keep arising
in the middle of the night.

You are your Spirit

Both the virtuous and the wicked
can only see
what their spirits let them.
For when a wicked man
explores a book of virtue,
then the spirit that dwells within him,
will arise and interpret
every virtuous word that he reads
into the words of wickedness,
regardless of how virtuous they might sound.
And it is no different with
a man of virtue,
who also sees what the spirit
that dwells within him lets him.
For when a man of virtue
explores a book of wickedness,
his spirit then too
will arise and interpret
every wicked word that he reads
into words of virtue,
regardless of how wicked they might sound.
As for their souls,
they are cultivated by the actions
of their spirits.
Thus, you are who your spirit is,
you are your spirit!

THE WORDS

The words of the Virtuous,
are full of love and peace.
They have the power to invigorate
any wounded heart in search of healing.
They are, in retrospect, the medicine
to every soul-wrecking life
that has been ravaged
by the words of the wicked.
For the words of the Wicked
are powerful enough
to disrupt the bottom of the deepest oceans.
They work like a magic spell,
enchanting all who listen
with the wounded heart in search of healing,
and as the wicked words pollute the mind,
they spread throughout the body,
infecting every atom that exists,
until they reach the wounded heart,
and tear its soul apart.
Leaving the wounded heart,
alone and breathless,
and in desperate search to hear
the words of the Virtuous.

Not in Vain

There will be a time,
mark my words,
when you will think of those lonely and yet soul fulfilling moments
of your life,
when you were ruminating on your life
while sitting in the cold and isolated cell,
sipping hot black tea,
and jotting down the first thoughts
that would arise in the form of a whisper
to your soul,
and although a good chunk of years
had been taken from your life,
and as soul-crushing on your soul that it was,
it was all worth living for.
For all of those ruminating years and days
that you have spent
philosophizing about life,
as you can see,
were not in vain.

Avaricious Men

The world is perfect
just the way it is,
although many men often say
that it is not,
because they cannot live
their selfish lives
the way they please.
And so, these avaricious men
do everything they can
to change the world that they live in
without understanding that
the world is perfect
just the way it is
without them.
Instead of trying to adjust themselves
to fit in,
these avaricious men
try to change by disrupting
all lives around them,
and in the process,
as they indulge themselves
with their greedy needs,
they destroy the way of life
of other men
and everything else that lives
around them.

NEVER FORGET

It is vital, I believe,
to our survival,
To never forget our dark past
along with our bright ones.
For it is remembering
those dark and bright moments
in our lives,
that will ultimately prevent us from
repeating our painful mistakes, and
being ungrateful,
and above all have hope
to recuperate from long lasting pain.

KNOW HOW IT FEELS

You want to know how it feels
to live in prison?
Then go to a nice restaurant,
order your food,
put both of your hands
in your pockets,
and just like that,
eat your food
with your eyes closed,
and after you are done,
have a waiter come over,
and search you for your wallet,
to pay for the meal along with collecting his own tip,
and do not forget to thank him
with a smile on your way out.

2021

Death

Once I accepted that Death
is just as natural as life,
living became not only easier
but much more fruitful to my life.
My self-realization gradually
manifested itself from denial to acceptance,
from losing people all around,
and every time when I would lose…
a part of myself would also be lost
with them,
and when I would grieve,
I would always grieve
alone in solitude and silence,
where I would start to appreciate death
even more,
for not taking the ones
who are still close to my life.
Who are still in my life.

2021

Despair

In some men,
despair grows like a cancer,
as they let it consume them
to the very end.
When I find myself in despair
and my spirit feels like
it is hanging on a thin thread,
to revive my gloomy spirit,
I start to ruminate on all of those
who once, I knew, have suffered
unimaginable pain,
and despite all of the internal struggles
that they endured,
overcame them in the end,
as they now live a fruitful life.
I try never to pollute my mind
with thoughts,
by ruminating on all of those
who gave up way before the fray
had even begun.
For they are like a walking cancer,
who will only drain
to the last drop of strength
from the revived spirit.

In Debt with the Devil

Next time when you ask for a favor,
from another man,
keep in mind that it has a price
of relinquishing your freedom.
To ask for a favor
is the same as asking for a loan from a loan shark,
except for one small part,
where you do not get to pay it back,
even if you do have the cash,
unless the loan shark
asks for his money back.
In the meantime,
you will have another man
hovering over you like a vulture,
watching and waiting for a convenient time
for you to relax,
and then nonchalantly swoop in,
to collect his price.
To owe a favor to another man,
is like being in debt with the Devil,
where you will not have a piece of mind
for as long as the devil
keeps part of your soul
as collateral damage.
Unless, of course, the devil will ask
for his favor back,
so, you can reclaim
the missing part of your indebted soul,
but what are the chances of that?

An Open Manhole

There is a reason why
I keep my mind wide open
like a cloudless sky,
look where I step
as I walk on my path,
nor do I look at others' paths,
or wish to trade my path
with anyone whose path
looks brighter than mine.
For there might lie,
an open manhole
far ahead of their paths,
that no men's eye can see.
Everyone has their own path in life
and the only ones who so stubbornly
ignore this fact,
are the ones who keep
their minds in the dark,
like a cloudy sky,
until one day they trip and fall,
into an open manhole,
where they will spend
the rest of their lives
trying to climb out of the sewage,
and in the process, tell to others,
the reason why
they keep their minds wide open,
like a cloudless sky.

Set in Motion

It's about time!
For the oppressors to feel the pain
of their own injustice
that they had set in motion
by their wicked deeds.
I am not saying it out of spite,
just to rub it in their faces,
because I endured directly,
so much pain and suffering
by the oppressors' hands.
But,
I have been patiently awaiting
for the Karma to do its job,
like it always has,
like it always had with me.
For when I wronged another,
I, set in motion against myself,
The Karmic actions,
which in time, caught up with me,
and punished me,
and when others wronged me,
I, from my personal life experience
dealing with the Karma,
did not think twice about seeking revenge,
but instead, only felt sadness
in my heart for them.
For I knew,
that their wicked deeds,
had set in motion, the Karma,
which in time, will catch up with them,
like it always has,
like it always had with me.
It is about time,
for the oppressors to have a taste
of their own medicine,

for it is the only way for them
to understand how it truly feels
to be oppressed.
I only hope for their sake,
that the Karma
that they had set in motion
by their wicked deeds,
would affect their lives just enough
to open up their eyes,
and make them realize
that how you treat others
is exactly how the Karma
will treat you.

2021

As of Yet

If, as of yet,
you have not been betrayed
to the point where
your entire spirit convulsed
inside of you,
and made you vomit
what you had devoured
earlier that day,
then you are not as important
as you might think you are.
Or,
the right price simply
has not been offered for your head
as of yet.

2021

THE CHICKENS

It should not be that hard
to grasp,
that if you wanted nothing to do
with me,
during my most desolate times,
then you have no right
to barge in
during the happiest times
of my life.
Believe it or not,
but many who once abandoned me
during my most soul ravaging times
Just cannot grasp
my simple request that I impose
so kindly on them,
telling them to stay out
of my life.
It is like telling the chickens
not to lay any eggs.

2021

FREETHINKER

If I was an Angel,
instead of a confused human being,
then I would not last a minute
amongst the Angelic souls
in the Heavenly Realm.
I would be cast out
for challenging our Father's ways
and trying to be a freethinker
amongst the followers.
I know it is an audacious thing to say,
especially for an insignificant, confused,
guilty with pleasures human soul like me,
who struggles inconceivably to be
recognized as a freethinker
amongst the other human beings
dwelling with me
in the Earthly Realm,
but I would rather be
this insignificant, confused,
guilty with pleasures human being
who is always full of doubts and regrets,
and who gets to challenge freely
our Father's ways,
and ruminate insatiably on life
like any virtuous freethinker,
who are destined to do with all their hearts
without being cast out.
For I know if I was an Angel,
looking down from the Heavenly Realm
upon the confused human souls,
I would have envied them all
and wished myself to be one of them
with that ignorant, adventurous,
innocent mind set
that gets to roam the lands freely like the spirit wind,

ruminate insatiably on life,
and challenge our Father's ways
like any virtuous freethinkers
are destined to do with all their hearts
without being cast out.
But the best part of being
this insignificant, confused,
guilty with pleasures human being
with the mind that was never destined
to grasp all that
Our Creator says and does,
is that in the end,
I would bear no fault
for being ignorant
with my thoughts, words, and actions,
for it was our Maker's designed plan
to have human souls search,
until they find a way
to light a candle in the dark cave,
without any matches.

2021

My Animal Instinct

Living amongst the enemies
was like trying to survive
alone in the wilderness
amongst the wild animals,
where I quickly had to learn
before it was too late,
that compassion, kindness, forgiveness
and docile behavior
was exactly what will turn me
into a well-done steak,
in the place where darkness consumes the light,
rules over the day and night,
then the only way that is left to survive
is to be one with the darkness.
For when I was living alone
in the wilderness,
heavily breathing in the darkness
into my soul,
I would force myself to silence
every human part
that made me who
My true Self was,
so, I could awaken the hidden
animal instinct that lives in each
and every one of us,
which had been dormant within the Self of me
for long enough.
The animal instinct that sleeps within
each and everyone of us,
is like a hibernating grizzly bear for me,
who comes to life
when my true Self
is desperately striving to survive
amongst the awakened wild animals around me.
It turns my guts inside out.

Makes me want to vomit
what my bear had earlier devoured,
when I have to force myself
to tap into my inner nature once again
and awaken the hidden animal instinct within me,
whose Self takes over, dominating,
and puts it-Self before the others
including me.
For the bear that lives inside of me
knows better than I do
that everything that human beings'
animal instinct says and does
is always for the Self.
For when it is not about the Self,
then it becomes about someone else
who is building one's strength
to use against you one day.
And when it stands before you!
To face you!
Your survival becomes slim to none.
In the places as dark as the night,
survival for all the awakened animals
is all there is.
For my awakened animal, the Grizzly bear,
survival rests purely on the strong
who have no compassion, kindness, forgiveness,
nor docile behavior,
and most importantly, it rests on the foolish,
who will awaken my Grizzly bear
from its hibernation
with a jar of honey in their hands.

2021

Folks Like Me

How can you possibly understand
folks like me
when you have never crossed the same streets,
walked on the similar paths,
nor ever lived amongst folks
with fractured souls and broken hearts.
How can you possibly understand
folks like me,
when you were born
with a silver spoon in your mouth,
while folks like me
were born with the crack pipe
in their mouths,
and when right from the start,
you walked on the bright light streets
paved with golden cobblestones,
with your head held high
admiring a full blue moon
with the sparkling stars in the sky,
while folks like me
crawled on their knees
looking for a way to survive
like blind cockroaches.
How can you possibly understand
folks like me,
when all you ever did
was look down on folks like me?

RED

Red is the color of freedom.
Red is the color of blood,
of men who bled for freedom.
Men who spilled their blood
have the most cold-blooded job
that never seems to subside.
For only a handful are fit
to grapple with
such a cold-blooded job.
Men who were born with freedom,
do not know the true value of it,
not like the men who bled
for freedom.
Although, as much as they love to say
that they value freedom
with all their hearts,
they can never say
that they earned it,
nor appreciate it,
like the men who spilled their blood.
Not until they have a fight
with their entire spirit,
and endure the pains and sufferings
with their entire soul,
and bleed from their flesh
to their last drop of Red
for freedom.
And only after such a
cold-blooded fight
will they start to realize,
that freedom comes to those who fight
and not to those who whine!
That the whining spirits of men
who do not know the true value
of freedom,

RED AND YELLOW LEAVES

are always miserable
with or without freedom
their entire life,
and that most men's spirits
that walk amongst the other men
do not possess the fighting spirit
within them.
The freedom is like red blood
in men's veins,
that always has to flow.
For when the blood is spilled,
then it is lost,
just like the freedom
when it is not being fought for.

The Only Question

At the end of each day,
right before I rest my eyes,
the only question that arises in my mind,
is, "what I have done for others
throughout my day?"
How have my actions
impacted the lives of others
in a positive way?
That will make me rest my eyes
with a smile on my face
and pleasant thoughts
running through my mind.

FIFTY-THREE!

Fifty-three!
Fifty-three years.
Years without a peace of mind,
without being free.
Free to live his life,
like any human being
whose spirit still flows through his veins
should have.
For fifty-three years,
they keep him away from his freedom
for the crime…
Does it even matter what the crime is or was?
Whatever it was,
it was more than half a century ago.
Too long ago to even remember who and why,
except for those who still keep him
away from his freedom,
for they keep him out of revenge
and not out of justice.
For if it was because of justice,
then they would have had compassion, forgiveness, and understanding.
But instead, they are heartless
with blood in their eyes
and insatiable cravings
to see more pain from a man
who they keep
for fifty-three years,
away from his freedom.

When they Came...

When they came,
they came with an intent,
to colonize the minds,
exploit the bodies,
and control the way of life
of a group of people
whose way of life was different
in every way from theirs.
For their way of life
was to swim naked in cold lakes,
sing and dance around campfires
from sun set to sun rise for days,
fornicate during ceremonies,
pray to their Creator aloud
and only in their native tongue,
fast under the influence
of the medicinal plants,
and chant while being in a trance
throughout the night
when the moon was full
and stars were visible to their eyes.
And as they colonized, exploited, and controlled
their minds, bodies, and their way of life,
no one seemed to mind
to see this group of people lose
their way of life.
For their way of life was not
the way of theirs.
Until one day, there was no one left
from a group of people
whose way of life was different
in everyway from the ones
who came to colonize, exploit, and control.
And then…
…

RED AND YELLOW LEAVES

They came in the same way,
for the ones who did not seem to mind
to see a group of people's lives
being destroyed.
For their way of life
was also not the way
of the ones who came
to colonize, exploit, and control.

2021

Refined

Any men who strived
with all the essence of their souls
to become refined
in places where it was designed
to crumble the entire essence
of human beings' souls
and take and take relentlessly
until there was nothing else left to take
by the parasites with insatiable thirsts
who are never fully satisfied, of men
who did everything they possibly could
with what was left out
of their drained and ravaged souls
to become refined
of all the sins that they have sowed
before they end up
colonized-exploited-controlled
By the parasites with insatiable thirsts
to take and take relentlessly
until there was nothing else left to take
from the drained and ravaged souls
who strived with all the essence of their souls
to become refined.

A Melancholic Heart

The wretchedness that dwells within
a melancholic heart
is fickle like four seasons.
Since in the Winter,
it is cold to the bones
until the sun comes out
and warms the lands.
In the Spring,
it rains like a waterfall
until the wind disperses
all the dark clouds.
In the Summer,
it is hot like Hell,
until the clouds gather
and block the sun.
And in the Autumn,
the leaves lose their colors and fall off
until the winter passes
and the Spring revives
what once was lost.
A melancholic heart is fickle,
like four seasons,
with stormy weathers in between
that unexpectedly come and go,
and although
it knows but chooses not to see
that there is a way
out of its wretchedness
where the sun rays never shine,
until a melancholic heart
steps out of the dark
to live one season at a time,
the wretchedness will persist to dwell within.

You can have it All!

You can have it all!
I want no part of it,
of that life that you so desperately chase.
Day and night,
so, you could feel a little more free
from the day before.
You can have it all!
All that filth that you put in your soul.
All that material crap
that you crave in your sleep
and fantasize about it even during the day,
You can have it all!
For I do not want to pollute my soul.
For I have worked
on the Self for way too long
to submit so easily to the way of life
that is so meaningless
and self-destructive to my soul,
You can have it all!
Take it, take it all.
I want no part of it,
or with people like yourself
who cannot even tell that they are alive
even when they are still full of life.

Out of my Control

For the most part, I have control
of all the little things
that I do throughout the day
to fill the void in my heart
caused by grief and pain.
But when it comes to transformation
of the entire essence of my soul,
then it is a higher power
who has all control.
All the little things
that I do throughout the day,
it shows to my Creator
A man that I am
A man that I strive to become.
Everything else beside that
is out of my control.
I just step back
and let the Creator
do the rest of the work.

Drop Your Act

You can drop your act,
pretending to have me
in your thoughts.
When the only time
that my name comes up
is when you are drunk,
out of your mind,
or high like a kite.
So, the least you can do
for both of our sakes
is drop your act,
and be honest with me
even if
you cannot be with yourself.

2021

Alone

Who knew that today
will be the day
of my forty-second birthday,
celebrating once again alone.
Who knew that today
will be two days away
from my twenty-first year
of me being alone
for half of my life.
But in all honesty,
I have always been alone,
way before I understood
what loneliness was even like.
For I did feel it all the time
in my black heart,
I just did not know
what it was I felt,
until I started celebrating
my birthdays all by myself.

2021

A Blessing

There was never enough time
in my life
to fulfill all of my dreams
and by the time
I realized that disappointing fact,
I already lost half
of my precious life,
and not to sound too melancholic
and melodramatic,
but quite on the contrary to that.
For my self-realization
turned out to be a blessing,
since I came to my senses
while there was still
more than just a full breath
left in my lungs.

2021

How can you say

How can you say
that you know me?
That you trust me?
When you have not seen me
in years?
I know,
I do not trust you!
For I have seen how people change
beyond recognition
in days.
Never mind what life
can do to a man
in years.

2021

ARTEM VASKANYAN

THE BEST YEARS

A man who spent half of his life
behind the prison walls
once said to me,
that he had spent
the best years of his life
without the light.
I do not know why he said
these gloomy words to me.
Was he looking for a hug
or some kind of sympathy?
But he did not get
any of it from me.
Only that I wholeheartedly
disagreed with him
on that gloomy subject.
For I too have spent
half my life without the light,
and what I came to realize
is that
the best years of my life
are still ahead of me.
And if any man
who climbed out of the dark
incapable of seeing the light,
and the best years ahead of him
the way I see it through my eyes,
then all he has ahead of him
are the worst years of his life
and darkness all around him.

Ground of Belief

Human nature consists of doubt,
and it is because of this crucial component
that it becomes that much harder
to develop a genuine belief in the Creator.
A belief in the Creator
that takes too quick,
too easy to attain,
does not have a solid foundation.
The easier it is to attain
a belief in the Creator,
the easier it will be to lose it.
Any spiritual growth that does not involve
time, sweat, despair, and even spilled blood,
does not have a change to grow.
The more there is doubt in a man
the harder he will strive to develop
what he so adamantly searches for,
since once he finds
what he was looking for,
and his doubts are manifested into a belief,
his foundation will become solid,
and no doubts that rise up will ever
shake his ground of belief.

The Trash

I guess you turned out to be
exactly like one of those
who wants what others have.
For when it was available for you
to have in your life,
you did not even bother to think twice
to turn your back,
and take what you had in your life
all for granted,
until a grateful stranger passed by and saw
that what he was looking for all his life
was right in front of his two sparkling eyes
laying in the garbage can,
discarded like some trash.
As he grabbed it just as quickly as he saw,
it disappeared forever out of your sight,
and now that it no longer is in your life,
to bring it back at any price,
you crave it more
then a garbage can craves the trash.

Ignorance

Seeing ignorance arise in others,
for some mysterious reason,
has always intrigued me.
I suppose it was because
it was always different for everyone,
just as it is for me.
Some, because of ignorance,
could not even admit to themselves
that it was a pile of feces they smell,
even if they were standing in it
up to their neck.
Others, because of ignorance,
could not even see the real treasure,
even if it was in front of their eyes displayed
their whole life.
Ignorance, I suppose, is different for everyone,
and that every man is ignorant,
only on a different level.

The Vagabond

If you would've seen me, really seen me,
then you would've probably kept passing me by,
for I am dressed in shabby clothes
that only a vagabond would wear in his life,
but this is because,
your impression of people first lies in
seeing them externally and not internally,
and this is why most folks do not ever get a chance
to meet in their lives
someone who values the internal growth
more than the external one.
Externally, I feel like a poor man,
or more like a vagabond to be exact,
but internally, I feel like a wealthy man
who was born with a silver spoon in his mouth.
And when I pass by other folks,
I only look into their eyes
where the soul of these folks internally lies.

2022

My heart lied

It seems to me that my heart lied,
making me believe for a very long time
that my true happiness had lain in feeling prosperous,
from fulfilling all that my deceitful heart desired.
And the more I granted the wishes of my heart's desires,
the more I became self-absorbed,
and the more my mind became engulfed by the dark cloud,
from failing to see what is more valuable to my life,
besides making my deceitful heart fully satisfied.
It was the day when I brought to fruition,
all of what my heart greedily desired,
that I realized, with great sadness in my soul,
that I have been for a very long time…deceived,
by my own ungrateful, dissatisfied, deceitful heart.
Since no matter what I did or do,
the cravings of my heart for more never did subside.
They only grew thirstier and hungrier with each fulfilled desire.
It seems that following my heart was not a smart thing to do,
for if the heart is deceitful, like mine is,
then it will only ask you to do
what is only best for it, and never for you.

2022

FATE

When I was young,
I, like a fortune teller,
saw myself in a crystal ball,
where I, somewhere down the road,
ended up on one of the two
most toxic roads known to a man,
heading to Prison or heading to my Doom.
I guess my crestfallen fate
had pity on me in the end.
For it chose a road on my behalf
that led me straight to Prison.
Grateful, I am not!
For having fate intervene on my behalf,
since prison, as it turned out to be,
was just like dying and heading straight to Hell,
and staying there, as in my case,
until my epic prison sentence comes to pass
and the road to Hell begins.

2022

Outside These Walls

There is a cemetery not too far away outside these walls,
Where many men amongst the ones
Who were not even condemned
To spend the remainder of their days are buried there.

It is the first place that I wish to visit,
If I do make it out alive one day:

For I have met and known most of my life
So many men who have perished here
And now are buried there
Without even being condemned
To spend the remainder of their lives within these walls.

I wish one day to stand as a free man outside these walls,
In the middle of the cemetery to pay my respects to them,
And give a moment of silence to these fallen men
Who were not given a second chance in life like me,
To see themselves one day to be set free.

O' how grateful would I be
Not to lay next to these fallen men!

For God only knows!
How many times I came so close
On my darkest days in life
When I heard no answers on my prayers.

ARTEM VASKANYAN

Book II

Last Days of Winter

Book II Contents

Last Days of Winter. 82
Two Forces 83
Art & Faith 84
When the Moment is Right 85
Why!. 86
On the Empty Stomach. 87
In Complete Darkness 88
A Kind Soul 89
Screwed 90
Not Awakened 91
Looking Back 92
Prayers. 93
A Moment of Silence 94
A Great Day. 95
A Real Man 96
The End & The Beginning 97
The Path to Understanding 98
A Fool & A Wise 99
A Moment of Dead Silence. 101
A Thin Thread 102
A Powerful Machine. 103
The Missing Part 104
Perhaps I Know 105
Sooner or Later 106
Likewise 107
From Dawn to Dusk 108
Self-Reliant 109
A Coward 110
All I Did 111
Cannot Coexist 112
Feeble and Sluggish 113
A Slip of a Tongue 114
The Way the Rains do it. 115
Bitter, Angry, and Wicked. 116

Petrifed	117
A Particular Look	118
The Wall	119
They Just Don't Know It Yet!.	120
An Opportunity	121
Voiceless	122
Unrighteous	123
In Between of Being Alive and Dead	124
Quick Success	125
Mistakes	126
Strong-Minded	127
Brave Heart	128
My Zen	129
Not Like the Candlelight	130
When the Mind is like the World	131
The Monotony of the Prison Life	132
Without a Second Thought	133
Benevolent	134
Self-Reliant	135
In The Position of Power	136
Another Self of Us	137
Crippling Addiction	138
A Limp	139
Tumultuous Mind	140
A Winner	141
Deep Sorrow	142
Free Like the Bird	143
Crumbs of the Pie	144
Madmen	145
An Innocent Envy	146
The Easiest Debt	147
The Spirit of the Grizzly Bear	148
I'm Going Home!	150

LAST DAYS OF WINTER

Last days of winter are coming to an end,
and yet!
I have only seen once or twice of the heavy snowflakes
descend upon me from the sky,
since the winter was born this season.
What has the Mother Nature installed for us?
An enigma is for all of us.
O' how I miss to be covered in snowflakes
From head to toe,
and walking under the trees
that are dressed in white fur coats
in silence and solitude,
especially on the last days of winter.
and thinking quietly to myself with sadness as I pace,
the fact of how it is all possible
that I might never see a single snowflake
descend upon me from the sky.
For all the signs are pointing
by the Mother Nature to one crucial fact,
that I might never see nor feel the lovely snowflakes
in the near future,
especially on the last days of winter.

2021

Two Forces

A man of Faith and a man of Reason
are like Yin and Yang,
two forces in the same universe
that constantly collide
overall, that exists.
They are both in a never-ending war
with each other
that could never be won nor settled
by either one of the forces.
And although,
they both know in their hearts
that it is true,
before they even start to clash.
Yet, they stubbornly continue
to pull each other,
each to their own direction
without giving up an inch.

Art & Faith

Before a work of art is born
a conceptual idea first takes rise
in the heart of an Artist,
and as his thoughts persist to flow
they manifest into words
and then into a living art,
crafted by an Artist's own bare hands.
And only then,
does the work of art manifest
from a conceptual idea into an art.
Faith is just like Art,
for it to starts with a thought.
A conceptual idea that takes rise
in the heart of a Man of Faith,
and as his thoughts persist to flow,
they manifest into a belief
and then into a living ideology,
crafted by his own set of beliefs
and after Faith has been cultivated, nurtured, and practiced,
only then,
does the work of a Man of Faith manifest
from a conceptual idea, into his work of art.
Although their both works of art
have been completed in their hearts,
they are never fully finished,
they are only a beginning of their life's journey.
Since Art and Faith can be lost,
just as easily as they are found,
especially when the souls of an Artist and a Man of Faith
have not been fed with daily practice,
and since it is in all men's nature
to question all that exists,
it becomes even harder to hang on
to their work of art
that came from both of their hearts.

WHEN THE MOMENT IS RIGHT

When the moment is right,
say only once what has been on your mind
and say it well like your life depends on it,
and if you chose to say nothing at all
then let that be the end of it.
For if you bring it up
when the moment has passed,
then you will look like
you are stirring the pot.
and in the end,
Yourself will end up in it.

2021

Why!

Alcohol poisons your body,
drugs pollute your mind,
and ignorant people bring pain and suffering
to your soul,
and when one day, you decide
to break away from the intoxicants
that destroy your body and mind,
Then Why!
Do not you do the same
with the ignorant people
who torment your soul,
As if your body and mind have greater value
than your precious soul,
that essential part of you
that keeps you intact in one piece.

2021

On the Empty Stomach

Just like the food tastes better
on the empty stomach
at the beginning of the meal
and not at the end of it,
so, it is the same with
folks who do not have a lot and
value all the insignificant things
in their lives more than -
folks who do have a lot
and who take all insignificant things for granted,
unless they too have a meal
on an empty stomach.

2021

In Complete Darkness

When my life was full of light,
the darkness relentlessly crept in,
and when I fell,
I lost my light and began to dwell
in complete darkness all around me,
with hope one day
to see the light again,
and only then,
in complete darkness all around me,
was the true essence of my soul
revealed to me,
as it showed me,
what light could never do
when it was all around me.

2021

A Kind Soul

I waited anxiously for so long
for a kind soul
to come and free me
from never-ending suffering,
But as years passed,
and I have not met a single soul
who gave a damn,
the spirit inside of me
that gave me hope for so long,
grew bitter suddenly
and filled my kind soul with anger in return,
and as the anger grew,
it spread and turned into a living fire
within my heart,
igniting a hidden furnace in my chest
that burned like Hell, unbearably.
And the more it burned,
the more the pain increased
and the more I saw,
that I could spend my entire life
in bitterness and anger,
waiting and hoping for, "a kind soul,"
to come and free me, from never ending suffering,
or, I could have my own kind soul
that I always had within me,
Quench the pain
That had been tormenting me
For so long.

2021

Screwed

Everyone nowadays it seems
is for themselves.
All people care about is
how to fill their own pockets.
No one genuinely wants to help,
not unless there is something there for them
in the end.
Everyone complains how the world is unjust
yet, no one dares to intervene
and help a man who is next to him
down on his knees
with hands stretched out in alms.
Everyone nowadays blames everyone else
for not giving a damn,
and no one dares to say
that if you and I are the only ones left,
then we are both screwed for good.

2021

Not Awakened

There are moments in my life
when I come to the point
where I can no longer do any fighting.
It is the spirit that dwells within me
that does all the fighting,
for even when I rest
my Spirit is awake,
keeping me safe from all the wicked,
who constantly seek out the wounded
amongst the strong
so, they could use their poison
to take advantage of the vulnerable hearts,
whose spirit have not Awakened.

2021

Looking Back

Looking back while trying to go forward
never did get me far.
It only made me stumble and fall
and lose the path
that took me a whole lifetime to find.
Looking back while trying to go forward…
All it ever did
was consume my mind.
By the tormenting thoughts from the past
that spun my head
like a spinning wheel on a loom,
Turning it into a living Hell on Earth.

2021

Prayers

How many times do I have to pray a day
for my sins to be finally washed away?
I prayed, and prayed so many times a day
that in the end,
I felt defeated,
for the sins that I have
a lifetime ago committed
have not gone away.
I have prayed so many times a day
that my prayers are starting to sound
more like whining than praying
at the end of each day.

ARTEM VASKANYAN

A Moment of Silence

I spent my life in places
where I did not want to be,
with people I did not want to see,
and acting without motivation.
I listened to those
who had nothing good to say
and did a lot of good for those
who did not deserve it,
and at the end of each unpleasant day,
I felt as if there was
a tone of boulders laying on my chest
suffocating me…
not letting me breathe with ease…
And every time I gasped,
it felt like my last.
And the only thing that revived me
at the end of each unpleasant day,
was a moment of silence to myself
under the moonlight.

A Great Day

Today is a great day
for a revenge!
And not the kind you think about,
where one goes out of his way
to bring great pain and suffering
upon the ones who ripped his heart
out of his soul.
No! Not that kind of revenge.
For the one that awakens in your mind,
will only bring more pain to both men,
and above all!
It will weaken the relationship
with the Creator.
The revenge that I contemplate
does not even come close
to the one that crosses through your mind.
For my revenge comes in the form
of motivation,
That gives me drive!
That gives me fuel!
To further cultivate my inner nature
and grow the Self within me
in intellectual and spiritual ways,
with an aspiration to make
all of those
who ripped my heart out of my soul
realize…
that what they did
was a wicked act against a man
who did not deserve it.

2021

A Real Man

Ever since I was young
I understood what a real man
is supposed to be like
from my Grandfather.
I saw how everything that he ever did
in his life
was always for his family.
Before the light even appeared
on the horizon,
he was awake and ready for work.
Working six days a week
from dawn to dusk
for fifty dark years in the factory
for the Soviets
never scared him a bit,
but what did
was not providing for his family.
and when days grew darker
never once did he prey on the weak,
steal, or cheat.
And he always loved his family,
and his wife unconditionally.
Since a real man
is nothing without his family,
He is nothing without his family.

THE END & THE BEGINNING

At forty-three
my Father's path abruptly ended,
and two months right after that
mine gently began.
Nowadays, as I come closer
to my Father's age,
I think quite often to myself
how he must have felt
as his path was coming closer
to the end.
A son of only four years old
and another still crawling in the belly of his wife,
what will life be like for them
without his presence in their lives?
Who will provide for them?
What kind of men
will his sons grow up to become?
He must have been endlessly overwhelmed
with such ruminating thoughts.
He must have prayed to God
more times at night
than all the Prophets and the Saints combined,
begging God with all his crying heart
to at least slow down the cancer
that was soullessly bringing the end
to his path
for just long enough for him to see
his yet born son crawl out
and enter into this world.
I know God heard my Father's cries.
He must have!
Yet, He did not grant my Father's prayers.
Instead, what God did in return
was to give the end
a new beginning.

The Path to Understanding

The search for the path
to understanding
has pushed me over my limits.
It will not let me rest my mind
until it will fully satisfy
the vicious craving
that festers in my soul at night.
Now that I finally, I think,
scratched the surface of what appears to be
exactly what I have been searching for,
I cannot stop following
the path to understanding
in search of more.
It is as if I have become a vicious junkie,
who will not stop the search for his drug,
until he finds it
and holds it in his bare hands,
even if it means falling down on his knees
in dirt and mud,
and digging relentlessly and endlessly
to satisfy his wicked craving
that festers in his soul at night.

A Fool & A Wise

"The Creator does not exist!"
A Fool says.
"You have no faith!"
A Wise man says in response,
"You conceptualized your idea
to express your strong denial
without developing Faith,
failing to grasp that Faith
is what causes one man to say,
'The Creator does not exist!'
and the other,
'The Creator does exist!'
In the world where men exist
in perpetual cycles of pain and suffering,
where their flesh rots from old age, sickness, and death,
and where the essence of their spirit
is constantly being tested,
Faith is the only Creed
that can make a blind man see
the existence of the Creator
while living in the temporal world,
Faith is the Key
That the Creator left us with
to bring us closer to Him,
Faith exists in all men, even in those who say it does not,
for it is part of being a man.
Men who strongly deny the existence of the Creator,
grapple within themselves
to keep Faith in a dormant state
and from further evolving
to become fully awakened,
Faith is a Seed!
Planted in all men's souls
that every man whether a Fool or Wise
inherently has,

Faith is a gift
from the Creator
to strengthen men's belief in His existence
through endless cultivation of their precious souls.
Without Faith, all men are Fools,
for the human mind was not created to ever fully grasp
what was not meant for it to see.

2021

A Moment of Dead Silence

When a performer's act on the stage
comes to an end,
and instead of a grandiose applause
from the warm audience,
He receives a lingering moment of dead silence,
then that is how one can tell
that his performance
was one of a kind.
For he managed to mesmerize
the entire audience by his remarkable act,
like he had put them under a spell
that not a single soul dares to interrupt
the lingering moment of dead silence.

2021

A Thin Thread

For a very long time now
My life has been hanging on
a thin thread,
and I always thought to myself
how it must have been one of the worst.
But as time had passed
and my internal growth persevered to increase
I began to look around myself
with more vigilance, and realized,
How I was not the only one
whose life was hanging on
a thin thread,
and the more I looked,
the more my perceptiveness would reveal to me
how grateful I should be to hang
on a thin thread.
For it could have ripped a long time ago
and made my life a hundred times worse
than what it is nowadays.

2021

A Powerful Machine

The mind is a powerful machine
that always has to be in constant motion
even when it is at ease.
For when the mind is not used
the way it was created
with a drive to persevere
then it becomes weak and sluggish,
and as the ignorance perpetuates to stagnate in the mind,
like the water in a pond
is being trapped under thick ice.
A powerful machine as it was meant
for the mind to be,
turns into nothing more
than a junk of metal.

The Missing Part

I think somewhere along the way
I have lost a part of my soul,
for I cannot rest in peace.
I keep going back in time
in my restless mind,
trying to meditate on every dark path
where I once walked
with my precious soul still intact,
in hopes to find somewhere along the way
the missing part
that could make me whole again.
I have searched so far
for the missing part of me,
in my restless mind
in the darkest places,
where the most soul ravaging
moments of my life,
took its toll on me
and left me searching relentlessly,
but as of yet,
I have not found the missing part of me.

Perhaps I Know

Perhaps I know why the pain and suffering increases
in Old Men with each day,
for they are getting closer to the end
without their consent.
Perhaps, deep down in their ancient souls
somewhere along their way, they failed miserably
to fulfill their goals,
and perhaps their pain and suffering increases with each day
from despair and loss, because,
deep down in their ancient souls
they know they will never have a second chance
to fully live their lives
like they once dreamed to have.

Sooner or Later

Folks who rely only on one
particular skill
that they had acquired
throughout their entire lifetime,
sooner or later will find themselves
in unforeseen wretchedness from the obstacles of life
where the life that they knew will cease to exist for them,
and their particular skill
will become useless to them.
It will require great flexibility of their mind
where multiple skills will be required to apply
in order to survive
the soul wretched moments in their life
with their soul left undamaged.

Likewise

I do not know where my head was,
but it most definitely was not
on my shoulders.
For now, as I reflect long and hard
back on my life,
most of my precious time was squandered
on frivolous words and actions
with insignificant folks
who placed a price on their priceless life,
and I, because of my ignorance,
did exactly likewise.

From Dawn to Dusk

At the end of each nightfall
As I lay,
and try to shut my eyes
from a draining day
that left me barely standing
on both of my feet,
and as I lay
I only think of one enemy
who stands in my way
and who I try to defeat.
Starting from the first crack of dawn,
my goal always becomes
finding a way to overcome
the never-ending battle over myself
who stands in my way
from Dawn to Dusk.

Self-Reliant

I do not expect anything from anyone
and because of that
I never become disappointed with anyone.
The beauty and the ugliness however,
from being self-reliant,
is that all of my achievements and disappointments
are always with myself,
and I become my own worst enemy
and I become my own loyal friend.

2021

A Coward

What kind of a friend turns his back?
What kind of a friend leaves his friend behind?
A truth was finally revealed to me,
the day I lost my precious freedom,
and where I found myself,
in deepest sorrow, overwhelmed with sickness and despair,
and where I needed help the most
like my life depended on it,
because it absolutely did.
The loyal friend that I admired for so long,
turned out to be nothing more than a coward,
and I, like a coward, never could admit it to myself,
until the day when I lost my precious freedom.
O how true it all turned out to be,
when my friend was nowhere to be found.

All I Did

If I would have never revealed
a piece of my heart
then you would've never
reflected on your life.
All I did was merely what other poets do
after they have dug insatiably
into the essence of their soul
and found what held them back to grow internally,
and then, shared it with the rest of the world,
from their heart.
For what they found did not belong to them.
It belongs to everyone
who is lost and searching.
I never did reveal anything rare about myself.
All I did was remind you
what you always had and forgot.

Cannot Coexist

The wealthier I see folks become materially,
the poorer I see them become spiritually.
It is as if these two opposite qualities
cannot coexist with each other peacefully.
It is as if the urge for the materialistic cravings in folks
does not know its limits…
does not know how to subside…
For it always desires more
and in the process, hinders their spiritual growth.
It is as if this urge bankrupts' folks' spiritual growth
and destroys their potential to self-awakening.

2021

FEEBLE AND SLUGGISH

The mind that has been kept at rest
endangers not only oneself,
but also, the loved ones around it.
Since the mind that is not being challenged
in time becomes feeble and sluggish,
and when hardships suddenly arise,
it will not withstand all of the pain
and suffering it has to face,
instead of overcoming them,
all the mind can do is seek refuge
out of the turmoil,
even if it means sacrificing in exchange
for its escape,
the peace of mind of a loved one.

2021

A Slip of a Tongue

All it took was a slip of a tongue by you
even though it was meant
as nothing more than a practical joke,
somehow it turned into a revelation for me
and a nightmare for you.
Where a true essence of your heart
was suddenly revealed to me
by a slip of a tongue,
and I could see
what I could never see before,
the real presence lurking inside of you,
mischievously playing in your eyes.

2021

The Way the Rains do it.

It is hard to imagine
that where now deserts are
once were mountains of dense forests with rivers,
seas and even oceans filled with unimaginable life,
and some deserts had not seen
a drop of rain in eons,
only the scorching sun,
scorching to death all life away.
Thus, it should not be that difficult to believe
what the shamans say,
"If we continue to care for our Mother Earth
the way the rains do it with the deserts
then life as we know
in front of our eyes, will wither away,
and the sun will be scorching to death,
our life away."

2021

Bitter, Angry, and Wicked

The bitterness comes from being wronged.
The anger grows from not being able
to do a thing about it,
and then it turns into the wickedness
from doing and wishing wrong to others.
The easiest thing there is to
grow bitter, remain angry,
and then turn wicked,
is to do absolutely nothing good with oneself about it.
It takes just the same amount of work
to sow in the garden, and then
water the seeds daily until they will sprout
as it is to extinguish bitterness.
It takes the same amount of work
to harvest all the crops in the garden
at the end of the season,
as it is to extinguish anger.
But to extinguish wickedness,
it will take every season to sow and reap
for the rest of one's life.

2021

Petrifed

I'm petrified out of fear
to one day run out of my dreams,
the same dreams that give me drive
to pursue and fulfill
all that my heart wholeheartedly desires;

for I only have so many of them
as it is,
until there will be none left of them
in my life to pursue;
and how will I live my life then?

For the only reason that I
have not been entirely consumed
by my fears,

is that I still have my dreams
to pursue and fulfill
in the way that my heart wholeheartedly desires.

2022

A Particular Look

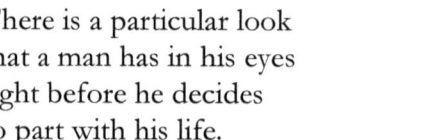

There is a particular look
that a man has in his eyes
right before he decides
to part with his life.
I have seen enough times,
these kinds of looks in men's eyes,
that I have become accustomed to them.
It hurts for me to see till this very day
when men pass me by,
with the same kind of look in their eyes,
and it hurts even more to say,
that when I see man who decides to part…
I have no right to intervene
between him and his faith
like I have done in the past enough times.
When I looked a man directly in his eyes
and told him lies,
that he one day will be free to live his life.

2022

The Wall

Whatever you think we once had
a long time ago had died from being apart.
The wall of friendship that we
a long time ago, together had built,
you had taken it apart brick by brick,
singlehandedly.
By blaming me for all
the misfortunes and disasters in your life
out of your own arrogance and ignorance.
Our wall of friendship had long ago collapsed,
just like the wall that we
together once had built,
leaving in the end, nothing but
ruins of it behind,
and rebuilding it will be impossible
for both of us,
for there is nothing left
worth rebuilding in the end.

2022

ARTEM VASKANYAN

They Just Don't Know It Yet!

Great sadness I feel for people
who gave up on themselves.
Who let their grief consume them to the point
that it transformed them into bitter, mindless men.
For they are now on their way
to becoming our tormentors
from giving up on themselves,
they just do not know it yet!

2022

An Opportunity

An opportunity for wealthy men
to succeed in life
is always there for grasping,
like it is waiting for them
to come and claim their price.
While for the poor men,
an opportunity very rarely arises
and when it does,
they have to be ready to take it into their hands,
before another hungry, poor man,
will snatch it right off
before they will even have a chance to hold it in their hands,
and if they do miss their chance,
they will never have another opportunity like that
in their lifetime again.

Voiceless

Violence is like a fuel added to the fire,
creating even stronger flames of chaos and disorder
amongst the voiceless men
who fall victim to the instigator's little tricks
as it further prolongs the pains and sufferings
in the lives of the oppressed and voiceless.
O how easy it is to fuel the flames of fire
of the voiceless men
who are exhausted so
from living their lives in the slums,
that dying no longer terrifies them,
but what does, is living in a way
that will not let them have a voice
to freely live their lives.

Unrighteous

A man with power
cannot wield it righteously
unless the Self of a man
had been cultivated from within,
righteously.
Oppressors are righteous by far
for they are just like the slave owners
who were just like back then as they do now.
Divide further the oppressed men
through chaos and disorder,
instigate fights amongst them
to create further bondage.
Use the divide and conquer strategies
to make the oppressed forget
who their real oppressors are
who keep them in bondage and control.

2022

IN BETWEEN OF BEING ALIVE AND DEAD

Only a man with freedom can be called a man,
everyone else without it
is something else other than being a man.
Something that is between being alive and dead.
A man who is in between being alive and dead,
who ignores the fight for his freedom!
Eventually will integrate with his oppressors
to oppress the lives of free men.
The oppressed and the oppressors
are like two different waters.
One is fresh and the other is salty,
but once the freshwater merges
with the sea water,
it cannot be drinkable again.

2022

Quick Success

If you become too quickly successful in your life
then your friends and even your family
will become your enemies out of jealousy
who are still struggling to make a name out of their life,
but if you become successful in life gradually over time,
then they will only envy you,
and you will get to keep them by your side.
But then the real question you have to ask yourself
is do you even want people like that in your life?

Mistakes

Small mistakes do not affect drastically people's hearts,
to the point that it motivates them to change
their inner nature.
It is only big mistakes,
the ones that give them nightmares most of their lives
that have the power to change people's hearts
along with motivate them to move the mountains.

Strong-Minded

I cannot afford to have luxuries while being shackled,
for when I get some comfort in my life,
I risk myself becoming weaker
and I cannot afford to be weak minded,
for the existence of my life depends on me being strong minded.
A strong mind comes a long way
from being prepared for the unknown
that mysteriously being placed on my path.
Every morning, when I get up,
I look at the chains that bind me
and at the oppressors that torment me,
and through the silent meditation
I prepare myself with the calm mind
like I am about to encounter death.
I visualize myself
running out of air to breath,
stepping out off the cliff,
being shot, stabbed, hanged, and even being sick to death.
I meditate in such a self-crippling way,
not because I wish to be dead,
but on the contrary to that,
to build a stronger mind
so, I could prepare myself,
to handle any obstacles of my shackled life
that mysteriously being placed on my path.

Brave Heart

Courage is not enough to master the Self!
It might be enough to master one's body,
but to master one's mind
it takes a lot more than a brave heart.
It takes compassion!
No wonder I searched for so long
in every place you could imagine
with the Self that was not cultivated strong enough
to reap what I had planted,
for my brave heart could never feel fully satisfied
from being truly happy.
The courage gave me drive,
to search in places
where my heart without it could never dare to trespass.
But once compassion gradually began to arise
from being more understanding
with pains and sufferings in the lives of others,
my brave heart and now my compassion
began to harvest happiness at last
with a strong and cultivated mind
from being mastered.

My Zen

My Zen is a way of life!
And it is as natural as my breath,
producing the fruits of self-awareness and self-reliance
from daily practice.
My Zen brings into my life
higher senses of sensitivity,
cultivates my soul,
nurtures my spirit,
and makes me see my true potential
in living my life as a human being.

ARTEM VASKANYAN

Not Like the Candlelight

Keep your mind
flexible like the branches
of the tree.
Free like the birds
in the sky.
Open like the oceans
around the continents.
Centered like the sun
in our solar system,
and not like the candlelight
that wavers to stay alive.

When the Mind is like the World

When minor and external matters
become a major concern to the mind
then it loses its concentration from dealing with
major and internal matters,
the only matters that provide
opportunity and prosperity to one's life.
The mind has to be
just like the world that it exists in
always becoming, always changing,
never stagnating, never, "IS."
When the mind is like the world,
it becomes flexible, free, open, and centered,
and the minor and external matters
Do not affect its growth.

The Monotony of the Prison Life

The more I spend my time
living my life monotonously in prison,
the more I start to realize
that I have never been free
the way I always dreamed of being,
I only thought that I was.
It is not a free life
that I crave for so much nowadays,
but for an interesting one,
the one that will captivate me
beyond my bewilderment.
There are plenty of pleasant moments
worth remembering,
during the worst times of me being locked away, because,
I found myself being self-absorbed
in my own creative projects,
in my own creative ways,
where I, for a very long time, found myself drifting
into the world of excitement and adventure
that keeps me free till this day
from my shackled life.
It is not so much being locked away
that nowadays torments my mind,
but the monotony of the prison life
that does.
All I seek nowadays
is not so much for a "free" life
that I always thought I had before I even was locked away,
but simply living one
that is different in every way
from the one I live today.

WITHOUT A SECOND THOUGHT

When a right moment arises
the one you have been waiting for,
seize it without a second thought,
and not before or after.
For seizing a moment
that you have been waiting for
at a right time,
is like taking the middle path to the enlightenment
and not the hard or the easy path
which will only make you be
too early or too late in your life.

BENEVOLENT

Men who boast endlessly of their
accomplishments in life,
their heart is not fully satisfied.
It is not at peace with itself.
It is not quiet and still
from all that they had accomplished
and because of that,
they cannot call themselves to be
as much as they wish, benevolent.
For a man to call oneself, a benevolent,
has to be confident, compassionate,
and truly at peace with oneself.
And when he achieves great accomplishments in life,
His actions speak for themselves,
Without a need for him
to utter a single word.

Self-Reliant

Being self-reliant for so long
Made me realize that,
Life is full of daily opportunities
Yet! Most men,
Because of their self-righteousness,
Are incapable to see it.
And so, they miss their opportunities,
To prevail over themselves
Because of that!
No one can ever make me successful
Only I have the power to do that!
For the secret of success,
I believe,
Lies in my own hands,
From being self-reliant,
From counting only on myself
And no one else in life.
For no one can ever be
More loyal, more trustworthy with me
Then I do with myself.

IN THE POSITION OF POWER

How interesting it is to see
a normal man
who is not that much different
from you and I,
turn in the blink of an eye
into an abusive, sadistic man,
when he is placed in the position of power,
and the more power that
this man attains
the more abusive and sadistic he becomes
and the more wickedness consumes
what was left of the virtue
within him.

Another Self of Us

When we want to see ourselves up close,
we tend to look into a mirror,
into the essence of our eyes to be exact!
To catch a glimpse of our spirit
come alive in us.
But if we want to know
the essence of our character,
the essence of our nature to be exact,
then we have to look for it
in our close friends
that we keep around ourselves,
since they are just another self of us.

Crippling Addiction

Anger is a disease.
A crippling addiction that develops over time
from not resisting the temptation
to further fall into an oblivion
of insatiable craving to desire more
of turmoil in the mind.
Anger spoils all self-discipline
that had been acquired over a lifetime,
making the equanimity in the mind
become unbalanced,
and vulnerable to further
being taken advantage of
by the crippling addiction
that develops over time.

A Limp

One day, I unexpectedly started to limp
and not from my old knee injury
that I sustained a long time ago,
but from me being around mentally crippled men
who, all day long, all they did
was to look for a way to avoid
how to do any work on growing their self-esteem.
And if I were to stick around
any longer around those mentally crippled men,
then I too, just like the rest of them,
would have developed more than just a limp.

Tumultuous Mind

Before it starts with the self-discipline, in general,
first, it starts with the discipline of my tumultuous mind
that is as thunderous as the dark clouds in the sky
ready to burst into tears out of the excitement from being alive.
The discipline of my tumultuous mind
is quite simple to grasp
since, it requires doing not a thing.
No movement
of the body takes place in any form or shape.
No thinking
of the mind transpires on any subject
No grasping
of the desired craving on any self-indulging thoughts.
Just sitting with the steady gaze
with only one goal in mind in front of my eyes
to follow my breath as it flows.

A Winner

You may think of yourself as a winner
after you fulfilled your selfish dream,
but when you live in a world amongst men
who violate all rules of the universe,
just to fulfill their selfish dreams,
Then without even realizing
you are just like the rest
of these men
who play the same selfish game.
You may think of yourself as a winner,
but when you violate all the rules
of the universe
to fulfill your selfish dreams,
then you are a loser
just like the rest of these selfish men.

2022

Deep Sorrow

When my sorrow comes to light,
it ignites like the lightening in the sky
right before it hits the tree
filled with life.
And then begins to gnaw at me
so deep that I can feel
the pain of my grief,
penetrating into the marrow of my bones,
bringing my entire flesh
and every part of my body's bones to shiver
like the earthquake shakes the Earth.
My deep sorrow grows heavier on the heart
with each breath that I exhale
like I have heavy boulders
placed on my chest,
sinking me to the bottom of the cold lake
like a heavy stone is dropped into the deep well
where the venomous snakes dwell
and have poisoned the fresh water.
My deep sorrow keeps me trapped
within the surrounding walls of a deep well
where I drown in its poisonous waters
like the sinking boat in the cold lake.
And every time I look up
with the last exhaled breath from my lungs
from the bottom of the poisonous deep well,
I see a light above me shining
in the form of a blue ring,
reminding me that my deep sorrow will pass,
just like the blue ring of light above me.

2022

Free Like the Bird

You often say you want to live
the remainder of your life
free like the bird
that you see fly in the sky,
Yet, you will not even open a single window
in your house,
like you are terrified of the slight breeze.
You live your life
within your own prison walls
that your crippled mind has created,
like the trapped bird in the bird cage
that has lived there for so long
that even when the bird cage's little door
is left wide open,
it no longer has the free spirit
in its soul to fly away.
Like the bird has all it needs
in its tiny bird cage
to live the remainder of its life
free like the bird it often sees
fly in the sky
from outside its open windows.
If you could choose to live your life
outside your own prison walls,
but only like a crippled bird
with both wings broken,
or, remain within your own prison walls,
but only free like the bird in the sky
that flies with its wings spread wide open,
then which one of these two would you choose,
I wonder?

ARTEM VASKANYAN

CRUMBS OF THE PIE

Those who save every crumb
of every slice of a pie
will never have in their life
a whole pie.
For they are so obsessed
with picking crumbs off the floor
that they miss out on the whole pie
that is set for them on the table.

Madmen

Those who are threatened
by nothing and no one in life
are nothing more than madmen,
for it is only madmen who have no fear
in their eyes, and who
are not threatened by what is instilled
for them in life.

2022

An Innocent Envy

When you fail to live your life
the way your heart has always desired
then you start to subconsciously live
someone else's.
Someone's life that you have always envied
But as your daydreams continue to persist
throughout the never-ending days without living up to your heart's expectations,
they start to hunt you even when you are asleep.
And then, your obsession about living someone else's life
unexpectedly turns bitter,
and just like that innocent envy,
transforms into a jealousy,
where from now on, a resent is all there is
in the heart that failed to live
the way it always desired.

2022

THE EASIEST DEBT

The easiest debt was ever to pay back
was the money,
although it has a great value to many,
more than the priceless life in itself,
but to some, all it really is
is just a material thing
that can be easily earned in time.
Paying back the money was always much easier
than the debt that I managed to accrue
to those who sacrificed their own happiness
for the sake of helping me survive
the most soul ravaging moments of my life.

2022

The Spirit of the Grizzly Bear

There once lived
the spirit of the gray wolf
within me,
within an insatiable craving
to dwell in unwelcomed places
and roam aimlessly like a lost wolf
searches for his pack of wolves.
Until one day,
it had found what it was searching for,
and ever since that day
it never stopped growing, it never stopped growing,
until the human nature arose from desiring more,
and transformed the gray wolf,
into the spirit of the grizzly bear
that now lives within me.
There is a spirit of the grizzly bear
that lives within me,
and not of some wild boar
that snacks on truffles
and rolls around in mud when the sun is blazingly hot,
nor, as once of the gray wolf,
that craved insatiably to dwell
in unwelcomed places,
and roam aimlessly like a lost wolf
searches for his pack of wolves.
The Spirit of the grizzly bear
the one that now lives
within me
is one of the most ferocious spirit animals
that I ever encountered
in my life.
For it devoured mercilessly
like a jar of honey,
the wandering spirit of the gray wolf,
as it stands its ground stoically

RED AND YELLOW LEAVES

with all its spirit,
and hibernates in places
where I could bear it
with all my soul.

ARTEM VASKANYAN

I'm Going Home!

I'm going home!
To visit the grave of my father,
for the first time,
who passed away a long time ago.
I'm going home!
Through countless mountains
that stand in my way
between me and my home
like the giant prison walls.
I'm going home!
Through the lush forests
and on my way, I pick
the sweet-smelling violet lilac flowers
so, I could place them
on my Father's grave
when I come home.

I'm going home!
To a place that I have not seen
For many decades,
Since I was taken forcefully away.

I'm going home!
Passing by the narrow river
Where not too far away
My little home has always stood.

I'm going home!
And now I see it
In the far distance,
and outside my little home
I see my mourning-aged mother
By the cabin's door
Waiting to greet me

And walk me to my father's grave
Who passed away a long time ago
Before I was even born.

2022

ARTEM VASKANYAN

Book III

When Lilacs Blossom

Book III Contents

When Lilacs Blossom 156
Beyond My Understanding 157
One Day 158
Love Alchemists 159
Blue Ink 160
One Right Word 161
It is You! 162
Blind 163
Only Love 164
More than Love 165
Crystals 166
When Hatred Ceases .167
Before I fall 168
My Demise 169
At times I 170
One Thousand Years .171
Once in a Lifetime 172
Here and There 173
Passing Away 174
A Glimpse into your Future 175
The Day After Today .176
The Only Reason 177
Folks who Smile too much 178
Folks Who Talk too Much 179
Sacrifices 180
My Heart Beats 181
Life Through our Eyes 182
In Your Heart 183
Risks 184
In Your Eyes 185
Between the Darkness and the Light 186
Happiness is just like Water 187
Desperate 188
What if there was 189

RED AND YELLOW LEAVES

Fully Awake 190
You Call Yourself Free! 191
The Blue Oceans 192
The Only Way 193
Desolate Times 194

When Lilacs Blossom

It is only when lilacs blossom
does my heart fill with complete joy,
for it reminds me,
as it takes me back in time
to a special place where I
once, a long time ago dwelled,
with lilacs in my little garden.
On the days when lilacs blossom
I would spend every evening alone with them,
in my little garden,
admiring the violet, pink and white flowers,
colorfully displaying under the blue moonlight,
as they fill my little garden
with sweet smelling fragrance lingering around me,
until they fade away.

May, 2022

Beyond My Understanding

I wish I knew why
it is beyond my understanding,
that I am the way I am.
I wish I knew the answer
to my relentless questions
that will not let me rest at night,
so I could understand the inner nature
that dwells within.

May, 2022

One Day

I know that one day,
many years from now perhaps,
I will have to come back
to this unpleasant moment in my life
that as of yet,
I have not mustered the courage within myself
to face my worst mistakes
that will not let me live my life
with peace and calm.

May, 2022

Love Alchemists

I am not a scientist,
but I am an Alchemist.
For you and I have a chemistry
that is so similar in us
that when we combine our ingredients,
we create a recipe for love
that starts to blossom into red-yellow flowers
that only Love Alchemists
have the power to create.

May, 2022

Blue Ink

My hands are shaken
and not from the cold breeze.
My entire body convulses
and not from being sick.
My mind is in distress
and the tears in my eyes
are not from stress,
but from the letter written in blue ink
that reads:
"O' My dear son!
I have gotten ill, so ill that I
have no strength left in my old spirit
to come and see you in a place
that keeps you like you do not even exist.
O' how much I miss you
and dream to see you one last time
before my spirit departs."

May, 2022

One Right Word

When a tragedy suddenly arises
in your life
your true friends will come to light,
and you will start to see
which one of them
is exactly who they say they are.
For all it takes
is one right word
to transform the tragic path
in one's life
to a happy ending.

May, 2022

It is You!

I see my future
and it is very bright!
For it is you
who makes my future bright!
It is you
who I would love to have
forever in my life!
And it is you
who I dream to be in love with
for the rest of my life!

May, 2022

BLIND

Sometimes I say,
"Why can not people see me
for who I am?"
But when they do,
I ignore to notice them,
as if I am blind,
and not from sight
but from internal growth.

May, 2022

Only Love

Only love has the power
to heal the broken heart
and all the pain that was left
from being torn apart.

May, 2022

More than Love

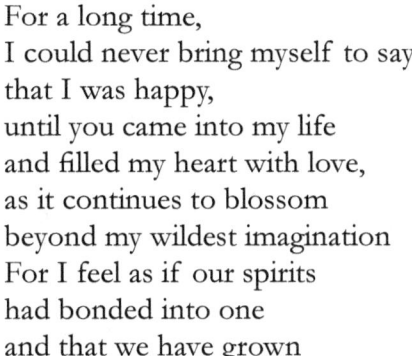

For a long time,
I could never bring myself to say
that I was happy,
until you came into my life
and filled my heart with love,
as it continues to blossom
beyond my wildest imagination
For I feel as if our spirits
had bonded into one
and that we have grown
into more than love.

May, 2022

CRYSTALS

The tears that shine
like crystals in your eyes
when the sun rays strike upon you,
are the glimpses of your soul
that shine from within you.

May, 2022

When Hatred Ceases

When hatred ceases to exist
it stops spreading
further down into the core.
Living life not only becomes easier
but also more enjoyable,
since I begin to see the world
and everything and everyone who dwells in it
not as the potential foe,
but as the living energy
that flows further down into the core.

May, 2022

BEFORE I FALL

Every night before I fall asleep,
I self-reflect on life
to see if I am in fact
walking on the right path,
and as I ruminate on my lingering day
that I have endured throughout the day,
and start to feel every atom of my body
coming to life,
my spirit lighting up,
my soul rejoicing,
and even tears appearing in my eyes,
then that is how I know
that the path that I am on
is the right one.

May, 2022

My Demise

I literally had to die
in my mind and in my spirit
to start living again,
to start breathing again.
What I inhaled before my death
was toxic, and it was fed to me
by the ones I held dear to my heart,
and that is why it took me so long to understand
what brought me to my demise.
I had to end up
on this soul ravaging path
that led me to my demise,
so that I could start seeing clearly
and not through my eyes,
but through my heart.

May, 2022

At times I...

At times I feel
like I have overstayed my visit
on this Earth,
For I do feel quite often
like I have lived more than one lifetime.
At times I wish
that my life was not as dire
as it has been,
and at times I wholeheartedly desire
that I would be missed
more often.

May, 2022

One Thousand Years

One thousand years from now
what will become of me?
Will I only be a distant memory
through poetry that I left behind
for people to remember me?
Will people speak of me
as a man who had endured too much
of the sufferings of life,
and that it was because of poetry
that I was able to live a decent life,
or will I be forgotten
as soon as I fade?

May, 2022

Once in a Lifetime

I would never tell someone
to not take a chance in life,
because if "I" did not
then we would not be together,
and "I" would not be falling
in love with you.
I may say no
to many things in life
but I will never say no
to love.
And how can anyone?
When true love only comes
once in a lifetime?

May, 2022

Here and There

Life is built on many failures
and a few here and there successes
in between.
My failures and successes
are based off my past.
All I can say about myself nowadays
is that,
my past is dark,
my present is bright,
and my future is brighter,
for my past does not define
of who I am.
It is my present
and a few here and there
failures in between that I encounter.

May, 2022

Passing Away

Everyone who I once, a long time ago knew,
are gradually passing away
and in the end,
leaving me stranded alone and in pain
in the world
that I do not see as my home.
O' how painful it is,
every breath that I inhale.
It pinches my soul,
from seeing the loved ones
gradually passing away,
Without a chance to say
how much I will miss them all.

May, 2022

A Glimpse into your Future

Do not be sad, even if you are hurting.
We all are, at some point at least,
and it is a good thing after all,
for what is life without it.
But the best part is,
and I say it with the utmost respect,
that God has great plans for you installed,
so great, that if you could have had
a glimpse into your future,
then you would have laughed electrifyingly
for the remainder of your days,
like you were high on love.

May, 2022

The Day After Today

Leaving unfinished work for tomorrow
for the day that might never come
has always disturbed me,
has always robbed me of my sleep.
For what guarantee is there
that I will have a chance
to complete what I began
before the day after today would arrive
since there is a very high chance
that tomorrow might not even come.
All the work that I try to fulfill
I do it in the present,
in the moment where I do exist
and not in the future,
since the day after today does not exist
and neither do I in it.

May, 2022

The Only Reason

The physical beauty,
the attraction between two people
in time has a way
to fade away,
and the only reason
that keeps them together,
keeps their love for each other alive,
is what they had cultivated within their heart
throughout their life.

May, 2022

Folks who Smile too much

Folks who smile too much
are full of agony,
are full of pain and suffering,
for they suffer internally so deep
that they dare not show their wounds externally,
For they think too much
of what other folks might think of them,
as if other folks have no pain,
have no suffering of their own.
Folks who smile too much
are deceivers
and they are good at putting up a charade
and at hiding their true character
that is internally in pain.

May, 2022

Folks Who Talk too Much

Folks who talk too much
are full of fantasies,
are full of unfulfilled dreams
that are dying inside of them
to be let out,
and the only way to release
these unfulfilled desires
for the folks who talk too much
is through the only way they know how…
Their trap.
For they do not possess the will power
in their heart
to take their dreams
and turn them into reality.

May, 2022

Sacrifices

The more I look around,
the more I become convinced
that my life is not as bad
as I have always thought it was,
although it is full of unfulfilled desires
that I insatiably crave
and on a daily basis used to pray for,
until I realized how tragic life
for many is.
My life is not great
and it has never been
the way I had always insatiably desired,
and I made peace with that
that I might never live my life
to the fullest as I had always dreamed,
but who really does in any case?
For what life is
with unfulfilled desires
and plenty of sacrifices in exchange
for being alive and spiritually well.

May, 2022

My Heart Beats

On certain days
my heart beats so peacefully quiet,
like the snowflakes drop on the beating drum
that I could hear a mosquito sneeze
from the room next door,
and on the other days,
my heart beats so disturbingly loud,
like the heavy rain drops on the beating drum,
that if the mosquito itself
was beating on my eardrum,
I would not hear a sound.

May, 2022

Life Through our Eyes

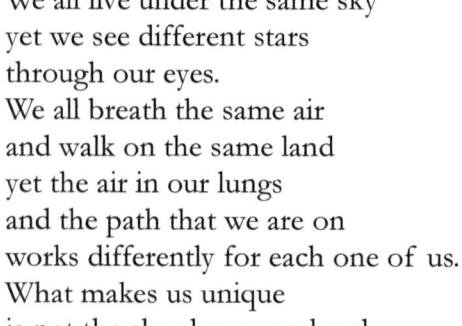

We all live under the same sky
yet we see different stars
through our eyes.
We all breath the same air
and walk on the same land
yet the air in our lungs
and the path that we are on
works differently for each one of us.
What makes us unique
is not the sky above our head,
nor the air we breathe,
or the path that we choose to be on,
but how we transcend
from seeing life through our eyes.

May, 2022

In Your Heart

Once the understanding
that you so desperately sought
was attained,
and kept in your heart
like a trapped prisoner
inside the cage,
than no matter how pure
your understanding might be,
it begins to rot and pollute your heart,
and what do you imagine does
the ignorance to your heart.

May, 2022

Risks

And what life really is
without the risks,
nothing more than a tasteless breath
that we inhale.
The risks all they really do,
increase the flavor to our tasteless breaths
that we inherited along with life.

May, 2022

In Your Eyes

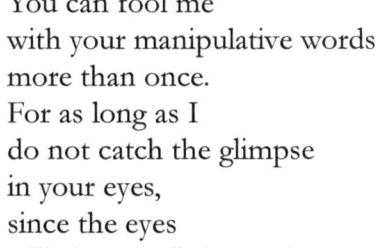

You can fool me
with your manipulative words
more than once.
For as long as I
do not catch the glimpse
in your eyes,
since the eyes
will always tell the truth.
For they are, after all,
the entrance into your soul,
where your true nature dwells.

May, 2022

Between the Darkness and the Light

I was never a man of God
when I lived under the blue sky,
but it was here,
inside this very cage,
where the sky is always dark,
that I started to pray
for the light to emerge,
and discovered between the darkness
and the light,
my love for my Creator.

May, 2022

HAPPINESS IS JUST LIKE WATER

I think that we all can agree
unequivocally
that none of us can survive
without water.
Yet, we find a way to disagree
that happiness
is not vital to our survival
as it is with water.
I believe that happiness
is just like water
that has to flow through us
internally,
since without it
we seem to wither away
just like the flowers
without a drop of water.

May, 2022

DESPERATE

The inner beauty as it seems
is the last to be noticed,
for we are accustomed first to seeing
what appears before us in the physical form,
the external beauty,
and if the external beauty
is pleasing to our desperate eyes
then we draw our conclusions
that what we see before us
is just as beautiful internally.
The inner beauty as it seems,
cannot be seen by an untrained eye,
especially when the eyes are desperate
to please the mind.

May, 2022

WHAT IF THERE WAS...

What if there was no hell, no heaven,
After life,
only what you create in your mind
to get you through the pain
in this temporal life?
What if there was no Creator, no soul, no spirit
that dwells within you,
only what you were told to believe
and the rest was all your imagination
that you dreamed in your sleep
that it would exist?
And what if there was everything
that you do believe in?
Then why do you still doubt it?
Why do you still live in fear,
like the Creator does not exist?

May, 2022

Fully Awake

At last, I found what I was longing for
and not in a place full of life and motivation,
but where most men do not
come out of it internally intact.
At last, I found what I was dreaming for,
and not in my sleep
where I roam like the Spirit-Wind
throughout the land,
but when I was fully awake
and internally in pain.

May, 2022

You Call Yourself Free!

You call yourself free!
Yet hatred is like a brewing storm
growing in your heart
and poisoning your mind.
Yet not a single thought
enters your heart
to forgive the one
who tore your heart apart
and sent you on a lonely path.

May, 2022

The Blue Oceans

Your eyes are like the blue oceans
that I find myself hypnotized looking into
and the more I look,
the more I am mesmerized
by your beauty.
That only a man who has fallen,
can easily get lost,
Like he is drifting
into the middle of the blue ocean
on a broken raft…

May, 2022

The Only Way

I will gladly trade all of my wealth
that I priggishly had gathered
in exchange for a peaceful life.
For the only way to thrive
is to have a peaceful mind
and depart from wealth that consumes the mind.
Besides, what wealth really is
without a peace of mind?
Nothing more than turmoil and pain,
and a piggish lifestyle.
For the more wealth I seem to grow,
the harder it becomes to let all go
and internally thrive in life.

May, 2022

Desolate Times

During the most desolate times
those who cannot find a way,
how to laugh,
do not know how to live,
how to laugh, how to cry, how to love,
when life is filled with joy.

May, 2022

RED AND YELLOW LEAVES

ARTEM VASKANYAN

Book IV

Dark Cave

Book IV Contents

Dark Cave 199
Chórniyi Vóran (The Black Raven) 200
"The Democratic Nation" 203
Tribal 205
Not one of you 206
Crops 207
Soul Wrecking Place 208
Rage 209
Cruel 210
Conquerors 211
The Prison Yard 212
Boots 213
Revolutionize 214
In Prison 215
Rotten to the core 216
Just another Form 217
A Breath of Fresh Air 218
Emptying my mind 219

Dark Cave

Deprived, abandoned and alone, I find myself
trapped like a decomposed corpse,
entombed in a dark cave,
as black as blindness,
where life that I once so desperately craved
with all my melancholic heart,
abruptly dissipated like a morning fog.
By a gentle breath descending from above,
that once breathed life into my lungs,
Transforming all, what I can only call,
into a living, breathing, inferno dwelling in my soul,
as I audaciously, with my bare hands,
dig to crawl out of my dark cave,
to catch a glimpse of light with my bare eyes,
so I could have redemption from external deprivation
that comes only in a form of internal innovation,
when the last drop of breath of hope
had been reaped out of my life,
leaving me deprived, abandoned, and alone.

May, 2022

ARTEM VASKANYAN

Chórniyi Vóran (The Black Raven)

I lived in a Communist country before.
I know what it is like to have no voice,
and if you do, then you would wish
that you did not,
for they will make you feel like you do not even exist.
I lived in a Communist country
where my grandfather fought
for the Soviet Red Army
against the Nazis in WWII.
Nowadays, the Communists are portrayed to be
worse than the Nazis
who caused millions of deaths throughout the world.
I do not like the Communists,
even though my grandfather did fight for them,
but back then, during WWII,
if you were not with the communists,
then you were with the Nazis
who were committing the genocides against the world.
My Grandmother's grandfather was sent to the G.U.L.A.G,
or like we the Soviet people like to say,
to Siberia,
for the crime of secretly operating
his own "underground" business,
which, back then, any kind of private business,
was illegal.
My Grandmother used to tell me
how life really once was
under the Communist Regime.
That secret agents in the black cars
that we the soviet people call,
"Chórniyi Vóran," (The Black Raven),
would unexpectedly show up by the house
and take her grandfather away.
Where he would disappear for many months,
and even years,

and when he would unexpectedly return,
he would be all covered in dirt,
skinny, unshaved and starving, and
with the look in his eyes
like there was no light in them.
"It matters how you live your life!
It matters how you survive!
Because your actions affect
not only your life!
But the lives of your loved ones as well!"
My grandmother would say to me,
quoting the words of her grandfather.
During my first few years of incarceration,
the F.B.I. came to see me for the first time,
which was almost twenty years ago,
and then the second time, a year ago, in 2021,
with the deal to release me,
in exchange to work for them,
(simply because I was from Russia).
And when I said No to them,
I understood how my great-great grandfather felt
when he too said no to the Communists,
who wanted him to work for them,
in exchange for his freedom.
When I was taken away from my home,
by the cops in the police cruiser
as once was my great-great grandfather in
the Chórniyi Vóran,
which at the time of my arrest,
I did not fully understand what was happening to me,
for I was too young,
but as time had passed
and I had grown into a man,
I self-reflected on life,
and realized how much my life resembled
to my great-great grandfather's
who too, was taken away.
I do not know if my great-great grandfather

even had a trial, but if he did,
then it must have been a lot like mine,
where the prosecutors and the police officers told lies,
the trial attorney did not put up a defense,
and the judge with a cold heart
rendered a draconian sentence.
And in the end,
all of this feels just like
another form of the Communism.
For I not only heard the stories
all of my life,
or seen this cruel unjust life
with my own two eyes,
but also live it to this very day.

May, 2022

"The Democratic Nation"

Why should I be ashamed
for being in prison?
When I was put there against my will,
by the corrupt system,
who gave me an unfair trial,
and punished me like I was not even a man.
And if this would have happened
to me in the Communist country,
then they would be the first ones
to call it a genocide.
For the so called "Democratic Nation"
as they love themselves to call,
do exactly what the Communist nations
do to their own.
Why should I be ashamed
for being in prison?
and for more than half of my life,
for the non-homicide charges,
when the government officials
who once in a blue moon get caught,
keep their government pensions,
with complete immunity for their crimes
against the entire "uncivilized" population
who live in the so called "Democratic Nation."
Why should I be ashamed
of my dark past,
even though it led me to prison,
when it is the only life that I had
which helped me to shape my moral principals
and keep them intact?
Shame not on me,
but on all of those
who so mercilessly, with a vile smile, buried me,
when I was young, uneducated, confused, lost
and without a tongue.

ARTEM VASKANYAN

Shame on the filthy wealthy, well spoken
and with a crafty tongue,
who commit crimes against humanity on a daily basis,
in the name of the so called,
"Democratic Nation,"
and in the end, never see the night sky
from inside a prison cell.
Why should I be ashamed
to tell the people
that I have been in prison for most of my life
and deemed to be an outcast
by the so called "civilized,"
who love to call themselves,
"The Democratic Nation,"
when everything that they touch
turns to pain and suffering,
which reminds me of the Communist nation
where I once lived when I was
back in the U.S.S.R…

May, 2022

Tribal

We are a tribal people after all,
for every one of us
is striving to belong
to a group of people with whom
we can share the same common goals
and dreams that will help us
find our path.

May, 2022

ARTEM VASKANYAN

NOT ONE OF YOU

When pain and great suffering
was afflicted by the oppressors
upon the people who you did not consider
to be one of yours,
silent you remained,
for they were not one of yours.
But now
that the pain and great suffering
is afflicted upon you,
you scream and shout, you cry and beg,
and pray aloud,
for someone to intervene
and save you from the pain,
and punish those same oppressors
who you once remained silent to,
when they afflicted so much pain
in front of you,
upon people who you once said,
were not one of you.

May, 2022

CROPS

Young are just like crops
that we plant in hopes to see them grow.
They have to be properly cared for,
with love and attention,
for if they are not,
then they will wither away
at the first sign of drought,
and in the end,
leaving us alone and in despair.

May, 2022

ARTEM VASKANYAN

SOUL WRECKING PLACE

Isolation, deprivation, dehumanization,
that is what the prison
is all about.
Soul-wrecking, soul-ravaging, soul-destroying,
that is what the life in prison
is like.
Angry, bitter, wicked,
that is what the prison
creates out of a man.
Despair,
that is what the prison
instills in a man.

May, 2022

Rage

Like a grizzly bear trapped inside a cave,
Like a wild dog being poked with a sharp stick,
Like a convict tormented inside a prison cell,
until one day, like a bird set free from its cage,
and then like a gray wolf roaming through unknown lands,
devouring what it can, out of rage.

May, 2022

CRUEL

Everyone deserves a second chance
that is what distinguishes us
from cruel animals.
Not giving one to another
will only set us back in time
to when we were acting just like
cruel animals.

May, 2022

Conquerors

It appears that evil
divides to conquer,
while good, unites to conquer.
It appears that
it has always been
and will always be
Us Versus Them.
Since, no matter how much They,
the oppressors portray Us,
the oppressed, to be evil,
as They look for a way to justify their reason
to condemn and oppress,
evil always finds a way
to divide, to Conquer,
while Good always finds a way
to unite, to conquer.

May, 2022

The Prison Yard

The prison yard is not
like any yard you will ever see
in your entire life.
For it is not only shared
by the convicts of all sorts
who come out to enjoy the fresh air,
amongst the other recreational activities…
The prison yard is good to run around the track,
use the phones if you have patience to stand in line,
smoke and drink the junk,
and also gossip like a selfish broad,
and gamble your family's money away
under the gazebo,
but, if you decide to cross the prison yard,
think twice! Think twice I tell you.
For it would be like crossing the minefield,
for it is covered with piles and piles
of scattered geese poop,
who fly to the prison yard,
with only one purpose in their mind
to take a dump.

May, 2022

Boots

Emasculated, striving to hang on
to their identity,
to their manhood,
as the soulless system
that they found themselves trapped within
keep their boots on them,
and the more they resist,
the more boots are placed on them,
pressuring them to give up
on fighting for their survival.

May, 2022

Revolutionize

I wish I could say, "Thanks!"
to all the wicked who had tormented me
and caused for my demise
in life.
For it was because
of their cold heartedness
that I was able to revolutionize
my life,
and transform into a man
that I could only dream
of becoming.

May, 2022

In Prison

In prison, depression roams like cancer
through the body.
It is on the high level amongst the confined
and there is no medicine,
there is no one to ask for help
or someone who genuinely cares.
Everyone is constantly stressing out
about something,
which in time turns into a chronic depression.
And it is no secret
that many turn to whatever they can find
to take the pain away,
that some guards smuggle in,
and yet, because of what is being brought in,
the prisoners are being blamed for it
as the prison administration takes and takes
cold heartedly away
the only sources of staying connected with the outside world,
the only sources that make them feel
that they are alive.

May, 2022

Rotten to the core

Sometimes the only way
to fix the justice system
that is rotten to the core,
is to flush it down the toilet,
since how else would you fix the System
that covers up the corrupt detective,
who gets recorded on the tape
stating to the suspect,
"If you will not confess to the crime
then I will plant a kilo
of cocaine on you
and bury you for life."
How else would you fix the System,
when the prosecutors do everything they can
to cover up the detective's corrupt actions
so they could drop their investigation
to bring him back on the force,
while the Judge, the so-called Honorable Court,
dismisses all the charges
and reinstates the corrupt detective
back on the Police Force.
The only way to fix
the corrupt Justice System,
as it appears to be,
is to flush it down the toilet
with everyone in it,
For it is the only way
to cleanse the corrupt Justice System
that is rotten to the core.

May, 2022

Just another Form

I live in a very beautiful country
where many people sadly
live like insects under a large rock,
because the government keeps feeding them
with lies
and making them feel ashamed
when they challenge their undemocratic ways.
That in the way,
is just another form
of the Communist Regime.

May, 2022

A Breath of Fresh Air

O' how I hate to fall
into a state of despair
where my soul begins to feel
as if it is being drained out of life,
from the unbearable turmoil in my life
where I am constantly deprived,
to take a breath of fresh air into my lungs
and breathe like a free man.
Each breath that I inhale, exhale,
is painful to my heart
as they burn my lungs
like there is a pile of burning coal of fire
exploding out of anger in my chest,
from holding on to so much—
that each exhaled breath breathes fire
from the bottom of my lungs,
and that the only way to extinguish my despair
is to inhale a breath of fresh air
like a free man does.

May, 2022

Emptying my mind

I love to sit quietly at night
and in the dark emptying of my mind
like a cup of water.
I love the sound of the rain,
especially at night, dropping hysterically,
on the rustling red and yellow leaves of the trees
with a whooshing sound from the gentle breeze,
and with my spirit I listen,
to the whispers of the wind arise,
--translating the celestial words to my soul,
that it is all a matter of time
until you perish,
but to flourish!
It is all a matter of virtue
cultivated by your soul.

May, 2022

ABOUT THE AUTHOR

ARTEM VASKANYAN

RED AND YELLOW LEAVES

As an Armenian refugee who migrated from country to country, since his young years – up until being arrested and incarcerated in the year of 2000- set him on a path in search of spiritual and intellectual growth, making him realize that without self-awareness living a fruitful life can never be fully experienced.